Walter van Laack

Lectures & Insights
(Vol. 2)

World views yesterday and today – What will remain and what will be laughed at tomorrow?

Author

Prof. Dr. med. Walter van Laack

Specialist for Orthopaedics & Orthopaedic Surgery, Physiotherapy, Sports Medicine, Chiropractic and Acupuncture.
Author of numerous books for existential and natural philosophy

Cover

Designed by my son **Martin van Laack, M.Sc.**
Master of Science in Architecture (RWTH-Aachen)

Translation

Translated by **Anneliese Wolstenholme**, Roetgen/Aachen (Germany) from the original German version "Weltbilder gestern und heute – Was bleibt und worüber lacht man morgen?", der Deutschen Buchreihe „Vorträge & Einsichten", published 2019.
Once more I thank her very much for her very kind and patient cooperation.

© 2020 by **Prof. Dr. Walter van Laack**
van Laack Book Publishers, Aachen (Germany)
www.vanLaack-Buch.de   -   www.vanLaack-Book.eu
www.Nahtoderfahrung.info   -   www.Near-Death-Experience.net

Printing & distribution by Book-on-Demand (BoD)
In de Tarpen 42, D-22848 Norderstedt (Germany); Fax +49-40-53433584
info@bod.de - www.bod.de

978-3-936624-47-2

World views yesterday and today -
What will remain and what will be laughed at tomorrow?

Based on a lecture given by Prof. Dr. Walter van Laack
on 22nd June 2019 in Fulda (Germany)

I was already confronted with death early in life. Initially it was the death of people I loved and who were very close to me. But I myself, too, came close to death at a young age and several times later in life.

I was, therefore, lucky enough perhaps to experience a number of incidents, which today are in general referred to as "spiritual experiences" or, in other words, "Extraordinary Experiences of Consciousness (EEC)".

Therefore, before I was even 30 years old, I felt the need to learn more about the subject of death – an otherwise unusual impulse for a young person. The world view in those days was – and it still is today – "reductionist" and "materialistic". According to this view of the world our death means the end of our existence and thus, of course, definitively the end of our personality. What we call our mind and our consciousness are accordingly mere products of our material brain.

In philosophy these are known as "epiphenomena". Accordingly, everything dies when we die, of course. The feeling of owning an "ego" and thus an individual personality is, therefore, purely an illusion and the term "soul" a sentimental religious fantasy.

My view of the world at that time came quite close to this perception, at least to a large extent, even though I had been raised with Christian values. However, my own "spiritual" experiences and early confrontations with my own possibly imminent death caused me to start seeking new insights which might cast doubt on this "modern view of the world": although at that time I was largely in step with this zeitgeist - I was never happy with it. How could I be when I had to accept that my belief in myself was basically just as absurd as my hope that after death something was still to come, even if this hope hardly seemed justified first? Basically, all religions convey this hope which is still hardly tenable under scientific scrutiny for most people. In the 18th century the German philosopher Immanuel Kant (1724-1804) stated, however, that religions are unable to really help us when we grow "more knowledgeable" in line with nascent "empiricism", today referred to as "natural science".

No religion offered him really useful insights. However, natural sciences are rightly claiming today to grow "immensely more knowledgeable in less and less time" and are thus causing many people to follow them blindly. This is the reason for the complete loss of faith for many people in the real core elements of all religions. One core element is in particular the belief in some kind of posthumous afterlife.

Such ideas are at best condescendingly smiled at today. In this respect, there is hardly a difference between the current scientific view of the world as presented to the general public by the media and my ideology in the 1970s.

Therefore, the following concept remains unchanged even today: "If you die you are dead".

This is the general consensus.

Therefore, I chose the provocative title for my book which was first published in 2003: "Nobody Ever Dies!" And my comprehensive first book, published 1999, had the title "Plädoyer für ein Leben nach dem Tod und eine etwas andere Sicht unserer Welt" ("A case for life after death and a somewhat different view of our world", published in German only)[1]. In spite of major advances in natural and also medical sciences I have not yet changed my view of the world which I expressed unambiguously then and which depicted a completely new and contradictory perspective.

On the contrary, it has even taken ever deeper hold. Meanwhile, I have become firmly convinced for decades that our "Self" is no mere illusion and that it exists in reality just like our "spirit" and our entire individual

---

[1] See bibliographical information on the list of my books at the end of this booklet

"personality"; I also think I can even substantiate this belief extensively and conclusively across the boundaries of numerous faculties.

Put very simply, the latter is the depository of all our personal and general experiences, all our thoughts, feelings, emotions and actions which accompany our lives as well as the extensive and very diverse knowledge we have acquired in the course of our lives. *At the moment we die "here", I call the personality which has matured up until then our "soul".*

The soul of a deceased person – from its own perspective – goes on living without any caesura after death which, unfortunately, must be endured by the bereaved. Thereby the soul starts a completely new life in a new world which is hardly realistically conceivable for us and which we can only describe roughly in the most general sense and yet it is a new world, level of existence or dimension which is nevertheless equally perceived.

Death is, therefore, merely a gateway to something really completely new.

All words which could only roughly describe this new world are inadequate. Even those people who, due to their own spiritual experiences, believe that they are entitled to claim they may have had a few short and fleeting glances behind the curtain, are not really helpful.

From a metaphoric point of view their descriptions must fall short since this new world is just as incomprehensible for us as for a caterpillar its later life as a butterfly – provided that in principle a caterpillar were able to comprehend anything.

This applies even to all those people who have had a near death experience while knocking on death's door. And it also applies to all those people who for more or less well founded reason claim to have special psychic gifts, and believe, therefore, they are able to make contact with deceased people by whatever means.

In my own well-founded opinion this new life awaits us all after our "death" and it is indeed a completely new life in a completely new world and, therefore, we lack the adequate words to describe it.

Neither do I believe that we will later undergo a (carnal) reincarnation into a new body on this earth, i.e. within the dimension we already know, as some far eastern religions and today many followers of esotericism assume.

My personal convictions have continually strengthened in the course of several decades, and this did not happen *although* but *because* I have been intensely pursuing this subject in all faculties which could possibly contribute something. On the one hand this includes all the major religions and numerous mystical traditions and philosophical views as well as the very colourful contemplations of modern esotericism.
On the other hand all verifiable phenomena, measurements and natural scientific and medical observations are of very special value, of course.
Time and again, however, I was able to observe that many conclusions were *biased* and they have been and still are being drawn without taking a look beyond the limits of one's own field of expertise. Furthermore, right from the start each new result is interpreted in such a way that it seems to fit perfectly into the general consensus of current world views. More often than not something unfitting is "made to fit" – or it is simply discarded.
My often expressed and authentic opinion is that our soul which represents our entire individual personality and which has matured in the course of our entire life up to this instance of death, actually survives our death. Of course it is understandable, therefore, that this view cannot agree with today's current view of the world. Should I be right, however, this also means that many of the "mainstream perceptions" which are all too often indiscriminately published mainly by the major media of our time, are simply wrong. I am convinced that the latter is true.
This is why I would like to demonstrate to you some former and also some current world views which are laughed at nowadays or will still be laughed at in the future.

Curious examples of world views

How ridiculous does it seem today that during the Middle Ages people allegedly still believed our earth was a disc. But actually people already knew more than two and a half thousand years ago that the earth is a sphere (e.g. Pythagoras, 570-510 B.C.). It was probably the Greek astronomer Eratosthenes of Cyrene (276-194 B.C.), who was the director of the famous Alexandria Library for half a century and who even calculated the circumference of the earth quite accurately. There are some people even today who seriously still believe that the earth is a disc – in spite of all counter-evidence[2].

Here a totally different example: in our latitudes we are a mostly Christian society which in its oldest form is based on the Apostle Peter. According to this tenet the Basilica of Saint Peter in Rome was built on his burial site. At least an eligible tomb is maintained in the catacombs of the basilica. Peter was crucified as a martyr head downwards and brutally tortured to death by the Roman tyrant Emperor Nero (37-68 A.D.) in the course of a systematic persecution of Christians following the great fire of Rome which was allegedly started by Nero himself in 64 A.D..

However, modern research shows that hardly anything is true in this story. Of course, like so many other rulers in history, Nero was by no means a saint but he seems not to have been a tyrant despite the assassinations especially within his own family, an almost common occurrence in those days in order either to gain power or to secure it (he is also said to have murdered his own mother Agrippina the Younger, 15-59 A.D., founder and patron saint of my hometown Cologne, who herself was busy killing undesirable contemporaries).

In fact he even furthered cultural life in Rome over a long period of time. He probably wasn't even a systematic prosecutor of Christians as is often purported. On the contrary, under Nero' reign, at least before

---

[2] Example: a telephone conversation of "Manuel" in "Domian", WDR-TV (2016). And the "Flat Earth Society" is an organisation in the USA, founded in 1956, that even today claims the earth is flat despite natural scientific evidence to the contrary.

the great fire, people were quite free to pursue their own faith as long as they did not proselytize in general public. When the fire erupted in Rome in 64 A.D. and destroyed large parts of what was then the largest city, Nero was staying in his summer residence in Antium more than 50 kilometres away by the sea and thus he probably neither laid the fire nor had in laid.

Of course, culprits had to be found afterwards to be made responsible for this catastrophe. This quickly led to pawn sacrifices among the Christians who were rather unpopular on account of their prevalent missionary activities. They were all publicly and brutally executed "in punishment". However, it is almost certainly true that Peter was not one of them. It is not even confirmed whether he had ever even been to Rome.[3] By the way, Rome was rebuilt by Nero soon after the fire, apparently even improved and more beautiful than before and even equipped with then modern fire precautions.

At this point, please allow me to draw your attention to a very interesting book by the theologian Enno E. Popkes from the University of Kiel who gave a lecture at my NTE seminar in Aachen for the first time in 2017[4]. If people had always believed the words of the Apostle Thomas and had not disqualified him in other gospels as the "doubting Thomas", early Christianity might have taken a completely different turn. Because according to Thomas the historical Jesus probably never saw himself as God but was well aware of his humanity. To be the "Son of God" seems to have meant to him what is true for all human beings and, of course, for both genders, and what I also believe, namely to be a consciously living creature of this universe and to recognise that behind all this there exists an indescribable, all-encompassing "divine unity" without "*whose*" unconditional love there would be absolutely nothing at all in this world.

---

[3] Varla, e.g. Prof. Otto Zwierlein (*1939), German historian, classical philologist
[4] Popkes, Enno E. "Jesus als Begründer eines platonischen Christentums – Die Botschaft des Thomasevangeliums, Kieler Akademie für Thanatologie (2019)

As a result, this gives rise directly to a definite personal responsibility for each and all of us. I will come back to this responsibility and I will emphasise it very clearly at the end of my lecture.

These are just a few examples and they will suffice here. Countless myths can be found throughout millennia and no one should think that modern natural sciences are the only ones which are immune to them. You don't believe it? Here are just a few examples of so-called "modern knowledge":

Let's simply start with the Big Bang Theory. This has been regarded as "secure knowledge" for a long time now and anyone who doubts it is just an eccentric and unworldly conspiracy theorist for many. So, what is this theory based on and how likely is it that this big bang ever happened?

This theory is essentially based on two observations which seem to support it. It was in the 1920s when it was established that celestial bodies further away from us show more red light than those closer to us. Red light has a low frequency. If you hear a vehicle racing towards you and past you with the siren on, you hear a high pitched sound when it approaches you, then it gradually turns into an ever lower sound when it goes past you and drives away.[5] The sound waves get longer during the recession.

The Belgian priest and physicist Georges Lemaitre[6] was the first to have the idea that, if there are far more "red radiating" celestial bodies in the distant universe, they must be moving farther away from us[7]. Accordingly it also follows that at some point in time they must have been compressed in a sort of primeval point in which the entire information of the cosmos as we know it today was already contained.

---

[5] Doppler Effect, named after Christian Doppler (1803-1859) Austrian mathematician and physicist

[6] Georges E. Lemaitre (1894-1966), Belgian Roman Catholic priest and astrophysicist

[7] Supported by the American astronomer Edwin P. Hubble based on observations

The creation of the world by God in the beginning seemed to gain a new, now even scientifically founded basis. This proposition was later mockingly referred to as the "Big Bang"[8].

The Big Bang hypothesis was born.

In 1964 a heat radiation was discovered for the first time which was distributed extremely uniformly over the entire universe, the (microwave) background radiation (BGR)[9]. Ever since the Big Bang is practically deemed an (assumed) fact; because now scientists presumed that the temperature of the universe which is just above the so-called absolute zero of only 2.73 ... K[10] was the result of a cooling process after the indescribably hot "Big Bang" of about 300 thousand years ago.

Today the "Big Bang" is estimated to have taken place almost exactly 13.8 billion years ago. Lemaitre's original and also partly religiously motivated idea turned into alleged "knowledge", especially since mathematical models were now being developed to support this idea. More often than not people overshot the mark, for example by inserting "constants", the constancy of which later proved to be fallacious. Neither were people afraid to "adjust" these constants and thus now and again reality was bent. However, this does not seem to bother anyone today. Furthermore, this seems to be a good way to generate money worldwide and many a Nobel Prize can be won. If renowned scientists pursue such myths – and in my eyes the Big Bang is nothing but a myth – and become the successful mouthpieces of their league, then all the others are quick to follow them, especially the many very influential and well positioned media.

Over the years, however, more and more inconsistencies were detected as a result of newly discovered phenomena and observations. Therefore, scepticism concerning the "Big Bang" theory began to surface. It seems, however, that it has meanwhile become a kind of

---

[8] Nicknamed by Fred Hoyle (1915-2001) British astronomer and mathematician

[9] Arno Penzias (*1933), German-American physicist, Robert W. Wilson (*1939) American physicist

[10] K=temperature unit "Kelvin", i.e. slightly warmer than -273°C. The dots behind the number are meant to indicate that this is an infinite number.

routine to counter such doubts: by recalculating and by resetting the parameters of supposedly fixed natural laws. Or something new is simply *conjured up,* preferably something that will be hard (or even impossible?) to prove. In fact, we know *nothing* about 95% of the currently known universe! The explanations are termed "dark matter" and "dark energy". Neither term is based on observations, however, even though this is not openly admitted and some horrendously expensive experiments have been started to finally find explanations. But in all likelihood neither "dark matter" nor "dark energy" exist.

Meanwhile scientists already look back nearly 14 billion years, a point in time close to the big bang and find that only a few million years after the event similar galaxies as the ones we know today have already formed which today are a mere few million light years away.

Furthermore, many astronomers were extremely irritated by the fact that the BGR is so immensely constant (isotropic) in the entire universe. It was good luck, therefore, when suddenly ever so slight fluctuations were discovered. Even though these turn out to be no more than a few millionths of one degree this seems to support the big bang theory for many people.

In a moment I will discuss alternative ideas.

At this point only so much in advance: The temperature of the BGR is with 2,73... K only very slightly above the absolute zero point. The dots following the number mean that it is a non-periodical and infinite (or expressed in mathematical terms: an irrational and not real) number or sequence of numbers. Only the first three digits are the decisive ones here. Of course, there are infinitely many more. Could there be a relation between the proven, extremely minimal fluctuations and the fact that this number describing the temperature of the BGR is not a real number and has infinitely many decimal places?

And what does absolute zero actually mean?

The fact remains that a minimum possible temperature exists, precisely this "absolute zero", a point at which really everything in the entire universe would freeze and thus come to a complete standstill. In the entire cosmos there would not even be the smallest of movements. Does this mean that possibly the BGR is the "minimum operating temperature" at which everything just starts to move, i.e. at which the first smallest dynamic begins to develop? Does this also mean that the BGR temperature is rather a "limit of feasability (LF)"? I do call it that and I will show you now that this limit exists more often than not and I might be able to explain why.

So what about the red light emanating from far away – or just moving ever further away (?) – celestial bodies? Scientists termed it "redshift". In fact, however, there are celestial bodies in vast distances which are definitely closely connected moving at different velocities away from each other and radiating completely different wavelengths such as red and blue simultaneously (e.g. different galactic nuclei, so-called quasars)[11]. Furthermore, the age of a celestial body alone even causes a change in the wavelength of the emitted light. Speaking of age: Long since stars have been discovered which actually seem to be older than the big bang which is supposed to be responsible for the development of the universe (e.g. HD140283) or entire quasar groups which, due to their enormous size, throw out all and any previous conceptions (e.g. "Large Quasar group", over 4 billion light years long, discovered 2012)[12].

Ultimately, all questions, for example what happened in the first seconds after the big bang or what was there before the big bang or what caused the big bang and why did it happen, will never ever be answered. All propositions must remain pure assertions and unprovable assumptions. In principle, some of these are non-physical such as the assumption that the big bang is based on an "infinite starting point" (singularity), since *infinity* is not a physical property. Nothing, but really nothing at all can give us any further scientific explanation.

---

[11] Example: *Galaxy NGC4319,* whose redshift seems to indicate an escape velocity of only 1,700 km/s. It is, however, connected with the *Quasar Markarian 205* via a bright band of light. The redshift of this quasar indicates a much faster escape velocity of 21,000 km/s.

[12] For lack of space here I must refer to my previous books for detailed descriptions and further examples, see my current list of books at the end of this paper.

Indeed there are numerous renowned scientists who do not accept the big bang theory. For example, when the professor emeritus for astrophysics at the University of Bonn, Hans-Jörg Fahr (*1939), was asked in an interview whether he considers the big bang theory to be an error he clearly answered with "Yes"[13]. And the American Nobel Prize winner for physics in 1998, Robert Laughlin (*1950), answered the same question by stating that the big bang theory was nothing but "marketing"[14]

Even with regard to the formation of the earth's satellite, the moon, scientist have been on the completely wrong track: to this very day it is believed that it is the result of a meteorite impact some billion years ago which ejected it from the earth or that is due to a planetary collision. Observations cannot confirm either. I would like to emphasise here as an important example that the ferruginous core of the moon is much smaller in diameter compared to the core of the earth. This alone excludes the hypotheses mentioned above. It is surely also remarkable that the radius of the moon is the earth radius multiplied by 0.273..., the acceleration of the moon on its orbit round the earth is 0.273 ... (cm/s^2) and its orbit around the earth takes 27.3 ... days against the background of our galaxy (sidereal moon orbit). Do you recognise this number?

Ordinal numbers and fundamental geometry[15]

Surprisingly we keep coming across the infinite (irrational, not real) number with the initial digits 273. Coincidence? Of course, this could definitely be possible, but so many coincidences all at once? And what role do coincidences play anyway? More about this later.

Let's take four identical circles, two neatly lined up next to one another and two arranged on top of them. We then connect their four centre

---

[13] Interview in the magazine P.M. 01/2009

[14] Quoted in the magazine "Der Spiegel", 1/2008

[15] All steps in this chapter are explained in detail and well illustrated in several books as e.g. "To Perceive The World With Logic" (2007) and "Nobody Ever Dies" (2015) and "Keystones of Our World – The Whole World Is Information" (2017).

points. Thus we obtain a square. This square contains and encloses each of the four circles including the one we started from. This circle is then termed the inner circle of the new square. Now we dived the area of the square surrounding the inner circle by the area of its inner circle. Or we divide the squared area of the square by the inner area of the inner circle. We will always arrive at the value 1.273.... If we reverse the matter and divide the smaller circle area by the larger area of the square or the smaller circumference of the circle by the larger circumference of the square, we will always arrive at 0.273.... In any case we arrive at the same sequence of digits 273....Remarkable?
I termed this number sequence the "limit of feasibility" (LF) with good cause.

In addition to this number sequence, which may possibly offer some important evidence concerning our world, there is a second infinite, i.e. irrational or non-real number, which I want to introduce here:
It is a number sequence with the initial three digits 618....
Here again the dots point to an infinite sequence of further digits – or should I express this metaphorically and say that the dots point to the minimal fluctuations they stand for?
This second number sequence correlates with the "Golden Section" (GS). From a geometric point of view it is the result of the potentially infinitely repeatable "continuous division" of a line segment into two subsections where the total segment always has the same ratio to the longer section as the longer section has to the shorter section. If the length of the larger section is divided by the length of the shorter section the result will always be 1.618..., or vice versa 0.618...[16].

If we now observe our world and look into the endless vastness of the universe, then we will notice that the Golden Section can be found repeatedly and everywhere. It represents the "optimum in our world"

---

[16] The fact that these and other number sequences can only be reconstructed within the decimal number system is completely beside the point, since they all are the result of geometric relations and thus independent of the chosen calculation system. Nevertheless, I pointed out in several of my books that natural phenomena obviously seem to be based on the decimal calculation system.

as I term it: For example, the petals of flowers are arranged in the same way as the coils on a snail shell. Humans and animals are "constructed" in accordance with this measurement, the distances between planets follow it as well as the distances between the spiral arms of our galaxy, the milky way, or those of a hurricane over the golf of Mexico. Architects construct buildings adhering to it, otherwise there would be no Gothic cathedral or the Parthenon on the Acropolis of Athens. Michelangelo painted his Mona Lisa accordingly and in music the perfect fifth follows this ratio within an octave. In mathematics this ratio is demonstrated by Fibonacci numbers[17]

In my book "Key to Eternity", published in 1999, I already suggested an "intellectual experiment" (fig. 1).
Let us play "creator of our world", with just a pencil and a piece of paper. The sheet of paper is a two-dimensional (initial) area. For our experiment we only need three specifications: 1) be as short and precise as possible, 2) multiply and 3) grow, in a strictly logical progression.
Starting point is a circle. Theoretically it could be ever so small. Since we put it on paper we could say it is a "finite point".
How can I define this circle exactly? The easiest way to do this is with three information points or else three "coordinates" which are positioned on its circular arc. With three (non-physical) pieces of "information" (born in my memory, spirit, consciousness or whatever we want to call it) I can now draw the first ever so small but always finite (physical) point, i.e. a circle. In contrast, the three information points, as mere coordinates, were of spiritual nature and are thus not finite or physical.

If I now want to multiply the first circle I draw a second one right next to it which has exactly the same dimension. In a strictly logical manner I construct this circle by drawing an auxiliary circle with the radius from the centre point of the first circle to its circumference. This crossing is the centre point oft the new auxiliary circle. Then we can prolong the

---

[17] Leonardo Fibonacci (1170-1240) Italian mathematician, see my books

line it by the same length over. Its end marks the centre point of the desired second (main) circle. By connecting the centre points of the two (main) circles I get a finite and straight line or "segment" (the first dimension). The initial auxiliary circle between the two centre points of the main circles intersects the two circular arcs, of course. Now I can insert "equilateral triangles" as a new geometric form into each of these two circles: each circle then contains exactly six of these.

In the next step I develop, again in a strictly logical manner, the second dimension, the plane. For this purpose I draw a third circle perpendicular to the connecting line of the two first circle centres. This is touching the top of the second circle. If I now connect the centre points of the first two circles with the points where the circles 2 and 3 are touching I get a "rectangular triangle" between these three centre points as the next and new elementary geometry of my "creation". The hypotenuse of this rectangular triangle also intersects the arc of the second circle at one point. This is a "logical starting point" for the desired growth. Through this I draw a larger circle around the first circle. Furthermore, this point divides the hypotenuse of the triangle into two parts in the golden ratio, the "Golden Section" (GS).

For now we come to the last step: I draw a fourth circle next to circle 3 and directly above the first circle. When I now connect all four centre points I generate a square inside the four circles.

At the same time this square includes each one of the four individual circles, as already mentioned here before. The starting circle can now as well be seen as an inner circle of the new square created by drawing the four circles.

Into each of the four circles I can now draw six "equilateral triangles", i.e. 4x6 equals 24. This could potentially be an important regulator in our world, since with the aid of this very simple geometric development, my purely theoretical game of creation, I already developed several important basic points, such as the Golden Section (GS) and the "limits of feasibility" (LF) based on the ratio of the circumference and the area of the newly developed square to its starting circle as previously explained.

II this is merely the result of a two-dimensional drawing on a sheet of paper in accordance with the rules of elementary logic.

Furthermore, a "rectangular triangle" was developed as a further basic geometric form. Moreover, behind my "physical activity", the simple drawing on a sheet of paper, there is also a *non-physical* element: such as the thoughts which gave me three important pieces of information at the beginning or (non-physical) coordinates for the first finite dot (circle, which is now physical).

The two now automatically developing *arithmetical* (mathematical) ratios "Golden Section" (GS) and the "limits of feasibility" (LF) which both appeared automatically, are *infinite* number sequences although they are both *finite* figures from a geometric point of view.

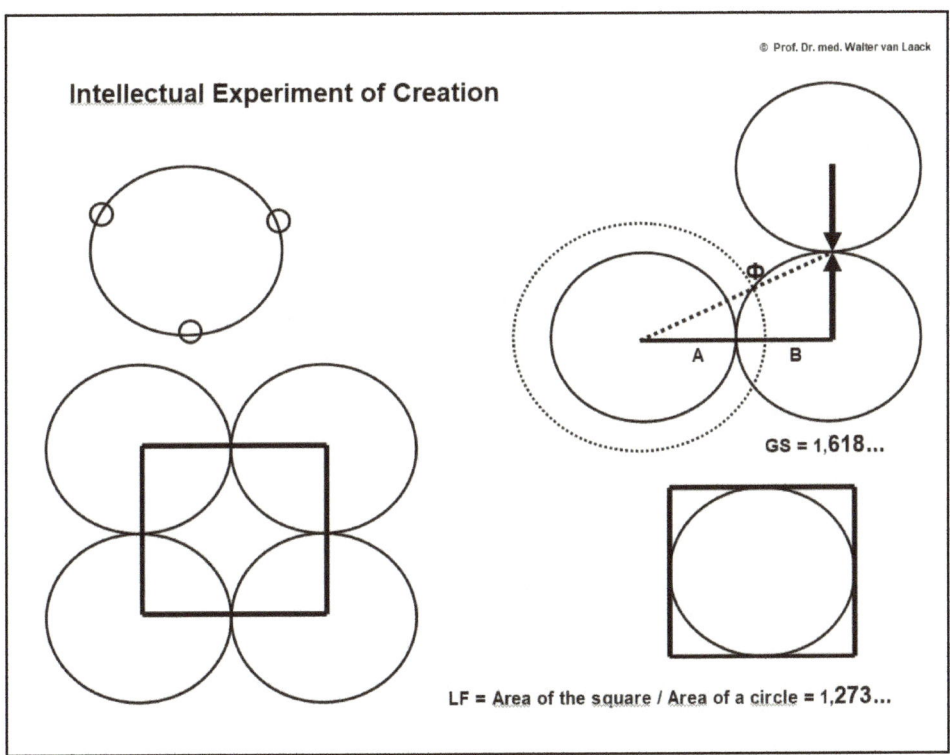

fig. 1: Summarising picture of my "Intellectual Experiment of Creation"

17

Let us take another logical step: Up until now all I had was a two-dimensional drawing on a sheet of paper and, therefore, "flat" or Euclidean, named after the Greek mathematician Euclid of Alexandria who lived in the 3rd century B.C.. However, in the next step we want to develop "space". We perceive space as being three-dimensional. But is that so?

If we develop space in a strictly logical manner according to the last steps of my "intellectual experiment" we can simply raise the sheet of paper vertically. However, we then have two sheets of paper which are standing perpendicular to each other. We could imagine these now as two interlocked "infinitely growing sheets" infinitely expanding into all directions. They would form a new and completely plane infinite space which, however, would now be in fact four-dimensional and can be thought as encoded by numbers.

Thus we get a spatial geometry which is infinite and flat.

The three-dimensionality we perceive is then merely a finite segment of a really infinite spatial four-dimensionality und only applies to finite bodies – such as humans and animals or planets and stars – within a really four-dimensional and infinite space (x^2y^2). Such a space can unequivocally be derived from Einstein's world-famous equation $E = mc^2$, which applies to inertial matter but operates with m = rest-mass . In reality, however, everything in the universe is dynamic, mass as well. That is why we have to square the equation and we arrive at: $E^2 = m^2 c^4$, where c is the velocity of light. In physics the velocity is "distance divided by time". So the dimension "distance" is in fourth power. Therefore, cosmic space must be assumed to be four-dimensional.

It is possible that our universe is a flat, four-dimensional and infinite space. All previously made observations support this notion.

Time would then have its own four-dimensionality. More on this in another article, since this would go beyond the scope of this article[18].

---

[18] For detailed explanations and further examples please refer to my previous books published in 1999 and later, see the current list of books at the end of this article.

The current view of the world as being a four-dimensional space-time continuum should, therefore, be ridiculed and the curvature of space, derived from this, would be wrong.

Of course, even the smallest massless light particle (photon) is diverted by a large mass, but there would be a completely different and also simple reason for this. We can find this in the polar-symmetrical existence of information and matter, as I already explained in detail in my previous books. A purely informational world determines the all decisive conditions for the beginning of the universe.

This informational world is also subject to an evolution in the course of unbelievably long periods of time which finally grows into a more and more outstanding designer of the whole world[19]. I will come back to the decisive and immanent "polar symmetry" in this world.

Matter and illusion

The famous English physicist Sir Isaac Newton (1643-1727) described gravity. For him these were mathematically precise, calculable forces between two masses. The British Michael Faraday (1791-1867) and James C. Maxwell (1831-1879) determined that there are also fields of forces in the cosmos which dominate space, the electro-magnetic fields. The German physicists Max Planck (1856-1947) and Albert Einstein (1879-1955) showed that in physics everything is actually *quantised*: Everything consists of particle. It follows that, accordingly, all forces and fields of forces should be represented by smallest particles without mass of their own.

In a telegram to Albert Einstein the Danish physicist Niels Bohr (1885-1962) once pointed out that "his particles" probably only arrived at their destination in the virtual vacuum of the interstellar space because they must simultaneously be waves. A medium such as air or water is required for the transport of particles. However, there is no such medium in interstellar space, a fact proven by experiments carried out by the American chemist Edward Morley (1838-1923) together with the

---

[19] I explained this in especially simple words in my book "Our Key to Eternity" (2015)

German-American physicist Albert Michelson (1852-1932) in the 19th century. Hence all electro-magnetic particles, in physics always shortened to light particles of photons, were attributed a *dual nature:* The "particle-wave dualism" was born.

Although the majority of today's scientists take this as a fact – it still remains a mystery. However, various experiments – such as the historical "double-split experiment" of the US physicist John Wheeler (1911-2008) in the 20th century – seem to support this postulate. The American Rafael Chaves and his team modified it in 2018: They inserted so-called "beam-splitters" unexpectedly late in their experimental set-up. These could then belatedly "surprise" single light quanta on their way to the measurement points and thus this supported once again the assumption of a particle-wave dualism. Furthermore: based on a purely reductionist-materialistic contemplation this experiment even paves the way to the notion, which is widespread today and assumed to be correct, that it is merely our decision to measure something – the what and when or whatever – that creates reality.
I consider this as utter nonsense.

All previous interpretations can also be easily dispelled here if we adopt a somewhat different though simultaneously extended perspective. This applies just as much to these results as it does to the especially seemingly odd "mystery" of interconnected or "interlaced" particles which are apparently connected with one another throughout the universe in a kind of "spooky" manner.
The physicists Erwin Schrödinger (1887-1961) from Austria and his colleague Werner Heisenberg (1901-1976) from Germany established that matter is basically pure illusion: Even in the smallest of atoms probabilities are the decisive factor. Something "solid" practically does not exist. Although every atom consists of a nucleus and a greater or smaller number of electrons, these electrons possess hardly any mass and they fly around their atomic nucleus at huge distances. There is no matter between them, just relationships or effects. Although these can be calculated exactly, no one can explain them. We speak of strong and weak nuclear forces which keep the atomic nucleus in the centre

together with its electrons around. No one knows how these forces are achieved and what they are.

A completely different force accounts for the weight of such an atom and it depends on the mass of the respective (finite) body such as the sun or the moon or the earth. It is termed gravitational pull or gravitation. The gravitation can also be calculated exactly as Newton demonstrated. But no one really knows what it is. According to today's physics which is focussed on finiteness and quanta, i.e. on "discontinuous particles" and does not even consider continuity, there should now be other particles which also provide this kind of force. They are sometimes termed gravitons and for decades scientists have tried to find them, without result, however, − and I don't think they ever will.

But that does not mean that scientists are not tempted to simply categorise a particle as something they would like it to be, even if some years or some decades later this proves to be utter nonsense. To me the "Higgs Boson", which was even pompously termed "the God particle", seems to be a good example for this.

And this brings us to the question as to what lends an atom its mass and thus turns it into matter?

In 1964 the English physicist Peter Higgs (*1929) had "just an idea". It was known that gravitation lends weight to the particles but it was unknown what adds mass to them thereby turning them into "firm matter". He had the idea that there may be a gigantic number of exceedingly small particles which exert some kind of resistance on the atoms when they fly through the universe, comparable to the resistance which you would experience when you walk through the water of the very salty "Dead Sea". The bigger you are the more difficult it becomes and the slower will be your progress. This inertia is supposed to lend the atoms their mass. Higgs himself found this rather funny as he said later and did not really believe it. But ever since his colleagues have been searching for it. In 2008 a gigantic, underground particle accelerator CERN[20] was instituted. In 2012 an extremely short-lived new particle was found there and termed Higgs-Boson.

Even though it was not found again in a size required to justify the term "mass"; scientists up until now have been satisfied with this explanation and Peter Higgs was awarded the Nobel Prize in 2013.

I believe, however, that it is not the key to knowledge and we still do not know what it is that lends mass to objects. The only thing certain is that every atom in the whole of the universe is just a tiny "breath of nothing". Although their internal cohesion is established by a force which is indeed exactly calculable it is, however, substantially inexplicable. But if the real knowledge about matter is extrapolated to all forms of matter in our world, then it becomes quite clear that even we humans and everything else must be in fact a mere "breath of nothing". Matter as we think we know and experience it is in reality just pure illusion.

We only perceive ourselves and all other "matter" in this way because we are created in the exact same way as everything else – and this applies also to all "extended arms" of our perception, such as microscopes and telescopes. But now it becomes much easier to imagine that a "complex spirit" or, expressed in a more general way, a "complex information cluster" could also exist in a completely different form of "physical illusion". Amongst themselves they would perceive each other in the same way as we do ourselves in "our own reality". For us they remain concealed, however. Esoterics sometimes refer to them as forms of "subtle materiality".

This might even be an accurate expression but at least it is understandable. During a near death experience people sometimes observe themselves from a bird's eye position as being a completely intact personality. From there they view their body which is undergoing the process of resuscitation at that point and they are extremely irritated.

Then it seems that we cannot completely dismiss the possibility I illustrated here.

---

[20] CERN = Conseil Européen pour la Recherche Nucléaire in the Canton of Geneva, Switzerland

Coincidence and Order

Esoterics claim repeatedly that there is no such thing as coincidence.
The past, the present and even the future are all co-existing times in our world and our spirit can randomly travel through all times when separated from its body.
There are even scientists who show a certain sympathy for the latter.
In my opinion this is utter nonsense.

The physicist Erwin Schrödinger also gave some thought to coincidence.
One of his intellectual experiments gained worldwide fame under the title "Schrödinger's Cat":
Is a cat still alive or is it dead if it is locked in a box in which a deadly poison could be released due to a purely accidental radioactive disintegration of some kind of material?
Many people think that this is only determined by opening the box.
This is the very moment of a "quantum fracture" or a collapse of the wave function. Some people even believe that this brings about two new "worlds" being created instantaneously: in one of them the cat is dead, in the other it is still alive. Basically, several billions of such new worlds could then be created all over the world every split second. In theory this might be a nice idea but I think it is utter nonsense.
By no means do I believe that as an "observer" we "decide" whether the cat is still alive or already dead by opening the box.
I think that it is pure coincidence. Such coincidences keep occurring at any time and anywhere all over the world on any level.
That is why in my very first book[21] published 1999 I already dedicated one special chapter to the subject of "coincidence and order".
In the physical world, in the world of the inanimate nature everything is first and foremost based on many coincidences.
So it is also a coincidence whether the cat is already poisoned due to radioactive disintegration or not when the box is opened.
However, every coincidence generates a clearly definable new and higher system at some time or other: it just has to happen often

---

[21] "A case for life after death and a somewhat different view of our world", (1999)

enough. After a coin is tossed one million times it will probably show almost exactly 500 thousand times heads and just as often tails. The same applies to the famous "Galton Board", a board with evenly spaced nails over which a large number of balls are dropped which distribute themselves in accordance with the "Gaussian normal distribution"[22]. A sufficient number of coincidences always results finally in a definite order. This made the French-American mathematician Benoit Mandelbrot (1924-2010) investigate the so-called "fractal geometry" within the context of "chaos research". And coincidences can indeed be really tricky when very many interconnections and networks appear suddenly which will need more detailed explanation later. Thus research into coincidence led to the − of course, hopelessly exaggerated − example of the wing beat of a butterfly in China which could trigger a hurricane over Florida.

Some physicists may object at this point that my assumption of coincidence is based on the fact that it would be impossible to know all the relevant parameters, such as the friction of the nail board, aerodynamic resistance on the balls or possible weight differences between the two sides of the coin, to mention but a few. If all these parameters were known everything would be known in advance and then coincidences would be ruled out. However, this is not the case.

Our world is based on the quantum world where everything is purely coincidental as recent experiments have repeatedly confirmed.
On the quantum level, coincidence is by no means just resulting from our lack of basic knowledge or our ignorance concerning interrelations or due to our unawareness of all the parameters. Rather, the result could not be predicted even if the entire system were fully known to the last detail.
So the cat in Schrödinger's concept is either dead or alive.
It is entirely left to coincidence and it is not the result of my decision as an observer. In physics, i.e. in the world of "discontinuous" and "disconnected" single quanta, a new order is created on a higher level due to a very high frequency of coincidences. And that needs time. This

---

[22] German mathematician Johann Carl F. Gauss (1777-1855)

is why it takes such a long time in the inanimate nature of physics before this new order becomes apparent and finally prevails.

However, over the ages nature provides a remedy by creating something completely new: It creates living, i.e. "biological", nature.
From this moment onwards everything gathers momentum, soon enough it even grows exponentially. And again a point in time arrives for new developments: Nature starts to interconnect its biological systems – at the beginning only a few systems are interlinked via rather simple connections, later increasingly more interconnections are created which become ever more complex by the creation of neuronal structures.
Hence, coincidence, the original major driving force behind this development, recedes into the background, very slowly at first, gaining more speed later and for us today this process seems to have become incredibly fast. The decisive factor here are the dramatically growing interconnections of biological and later neuronal systems for the transport of information. Thus evolution is striving to open up new horizons with an interactive system between matter and spirit.

Polar symmetry everywhere in the world

About two and a half thousand years ago, Chinese philosophy was already aware of a crucial basic principle of our world.
It is the principle of "polar symmetry" which, in my opinion, is so brilliantly depicted by the famous Yin and Yang symbol:

Two mirror-inverted flames are lying opposite to each other (polar-symmetrical) each containing one aspect of the other and "nourishing" each other. You cannot have one without the other.

Frank Wilczek [23] (*1951), American Nobel Prize winner for Physics 2004, once said: ": "The world is a work of art created in a very special style", and further, "I am particularly struck by the outstanding importance of symmetry."

There is polar symmetry everywhere in our world. Wherever there are finite spaces (e.g. living organisms) and finite periods of time (e.g. our lives) there must also be infinite spaces and time periods. This is exactly how it is: The ancient Greeks were amazed about the hypotenuse of a right-angled triangle or of the area and the circumference of a circle, since they are all mathematically infinite (e.g. the number π[24]), but optically (or geometrically), however, they are not. Later the German mathematician Georg Cantor (1845-1918) was not only able to prove that infinity exists in this world but he even established that there must be an infinite number of real infinities. We cannot imagine what the term "infinity" really means, we can imagine "unbelievably many", but "infinitely many"?

From all of this it even follows that only one single infinite number could contain all information pertaining to simply everything and everyone in this world at any one time. Incredible, but true! But when we are able to store huge amounts of information with only two numbers (1 and 0, binary system) on our computers and in the internet, resulting in 1024 (= 2^{10}) stored information bits after only 10 digits, then we are able to store 10^{10} information bits with one-digit numbers (0 to 9) after 10 digits and thus 10 billion bits.

Someone from Japan already calculated over three billion decimal places for the number π (pi) a few years ago. Even if some people still believe that this number sequence might be finite they are probably wrong: The mathematical constant π is definitely infinite.

Wherever there are *cyclical* processes there are certainly also *linear* ones. All finite solids have a cyclical life. They are generated, they mature and finally they decay. The sun and the earth, for example, exist

---

[23] Source: "DER SPIEGEL" 33, 2015

[24] π (= pi) is a mathematical constant defining the ratio of a circle's circumference to its diameter

26

for a certain time and then they will certainly perish. For us, this time span of some billion years seems gigantic, of course. But it is nonetheless finite. In physics this cosmic principle of each and every finite entity is termed "entropy". It is a measure for the gradual decline into disorder in this world. Everything will be destroyed sooner or later, the physical world always declines from a higher level of order into disorder.

This also applies to the life of all animals and to us humans, of course, since we all have finite bodies which follow the laws of entropy and can, therefore, only live in this form for a limited time.

However, where there is a *cyclic effect* due to decay and increasing disorder there must also be a *linearity* due to constant development and increasing order. We can experience this in ourselves, for example: While in the course of their lives from the very beginning onwards all humans start to grow old although it takes them about 25 years to become adult before decay starts to show, their spirits continue to grow.

Their (intangible or non-physical) personality matures continuously in a *linear* manner. This is no evaluation, of course, since negative aspects of personalities undergo this process as well.

And to grow in a linear manner does not necessarily mean to grow evenly and continuously. The "non-material" aspect still continues to mature until the inevitable end of the body which we call death. If then, due to physical entropy, every body comes to its end – it dies as we say – the mature spirit is at this point in its prime.[25]

Logic alone should make us ask ourselves whether this should really be all there is? Or, when "its" body inevitably dies, could the continuously matured spirit not stand at the beginning of a "new journey" to another completely new life after having undergone an imperative "metamorphosis"? I think this is the case!

---

[25] Dementia are no lack of spirit but rather a defect of the brain which leads to spiritual lack of access to this "type of computer"

At the moment of death, the spirit, and thus the entire personality of the "merely physically dead" person, has reached a state which I like to term "soul" following Christian tradition. And this soul goes on living.

Based on this firm conviction we must ask ourselves, of course, how we can imagine this, when the brain, commonly assumed to be the producer of the spirit – at least the undisputed organ necessary for the spirit throughout life – no longer functions after our physical death.

For more than 100 years now we have known that in the physical world everything is quantized. This is why scientists keep looking for small particles which may induce gravity (gravitons), which keep the small components (e.g. quarks) together in the nucleus of an atom (gluons) or which lend mass to all matter (Higgs bosons?). Even after having found an incredibly fast disintegrating particle which was, probably prematurely, supposed to lend mass to an atom: physicists remain doubtful.

I share the view that it is still not clear what it is that lends mass to particles or finite objects in general. And even though it has become possible to measure gravitation as an energy field which is active throughout the entire universe, gravitons have not yet been found despite intensified search, nor have gluons, the assumed adhesive particles in an atomic nucleus. Indeed, Max Planck and Albert Einstein were right when they recognised that the physical world consists of particles. However, the acceptance that it consists ONLY of particles is still missing.

Everything in physics, and thus everything in our physical universe, is discontinuous, i.e. "divided" and "disconnected". There is in fact no continuity in physics.

However, since particles could not fly through a nearly medium-free universe (quasi-vacuum) without continuity, a "particle-wave dualism" was invented, since continuity was needed.

This continuity was thus just created by attributing a dual nature to the smallest particles, the quanta or photons.

Of course, then continuity must exist in our world – every kind of life is characterised by it.

This raises a different question: Is continuity a property of the physical world? No, I don't think so!

Of course, in our world we have real continuity. However, as the real existence of infinity demonstrates it is also from "another world". Both worlds reflect the universal law of "polar symmetry". Again, continuity forces us to recognise the real existence of a dimension or world which is polar-symmetrical to the physical world. This world cannot be explained by physics and it does not comply with it. But of course it is just as real as the physical world we perceive.

Furthermore, it is in fact the stronger reality. It is the world of all "information" which undergoes a similar evolution as the physical world. In the physical world objects become ever more complex, in the other world "information clusters" become ever more complex. Put simply, it is the "spirit". A spirit which has developed and progressed in an evolutionary process then possesses such amazing properties as consciousness, emotionality and self-awareness.

The "world of an increasing information growth which gains ever higher complexity", or, in simple words the "spiritual world", is thus the *first* "real world" and also the stronger one which stands behind everything, and this means that ultimately everything emanates from there. For this it needs the physical world as a kind of expression and also for its own evolution.

For us the expressions "world of information" or "spiritual world" sound very abstract and so completely immaterial. But in fact, this world is not at all like that – this world is just completely different and can hardly be experienced with physical methods.

From a purely scientific point of view it has long since been indisputable that all the matter we perceive does not really exist and should be considered an illusion. All physical, i.e. all finite bodies, those of animals and also those of humans, are in fact nothing but a "breath of nothing".

The renowned German physicist Hans-Peter Dürr (1929-2014), a scientific offspring of Carl Friedrich von Weizsäcker (1912-2007) and Werner Heisenberg (1901-1976) once stated the following: "In the subatomic quantum world there are no objects, no matter, no substance, i.e. things we can touch. There are only movements, processes, connections, information ... (the cosmos) is an information field ... it has nothing to do with mass and energy ... this uncertainty refers to an underlying universal code, which is nothing but information ... matter and energy only appear secondarily – it may be regarded as a kind of coagulated, solidified spirit". [26]

And the founder of quantum physics, the German physicist Max Planck (1858-1947), even remarked in one of his lectures in 1918: "

I consider matter as something that is created by consciousness. All matter emerges and is only kept in existence by some kind of power which makes the atomic particles oscillate ... (we must) assume that there is a conscious intelligent spirit behind this power. This spirit is the origin of all matter ... "

Life and Evolution

So now is the time to take a look at the evolution of all life on earth and, of course, that of humans as well.

To begin with, we have to ask whether really all life as we know it here and now in its gigantic complexity could have developed over the course of half a billion years merely due to coincidence and the subsequent consistent selection of the "most suitable" candidates. Biologists today and also numerous brain researchers make exactly that claim. However, when looking for an answer, we should not prematurely disregard the facts which become pretty obvious, even when taking only a superficial glance, and which cast doubt on this assumption:

It took nature, for example, 40 million years to develop the hooves of animals. However, it took nature only a few 100 thousand years to develop the highly complex human brain from the preliminary stages found in our animal ancestors.

And although the prehistoric people of the Stone Age lived only about ten thousand years ago, which is the equivalent of about 400 generations, we modern humans are – from a purely spiritual point of

[26] Source: P.M. Magazine 05/2007

view – worlds apart from the Stone Age population. This is by no means a judgement; of course, the universal principle of polar symmetry applies here as well, meaning unfortunately: where there is much light there is also much shadow.

Similarly, if Darwin's dictum, according to which success is determined by superiority[27], each coincidental development of something completely new should already have advantages in the next generation which enable it to survive. In principle, something new must constantly be developed which proves to be beneficial right away.

Normally, however, a mutation, which might prove to be more suitable, needs several or even very many generations before its superiority comes into effect. Furthermore, it sometimes needs an environmental change to enable new features, which might even have been of disadvantage for a long period of time, to come into their own and become beneficial. It becomes especially difficult for vital peculiarities and mannerisms of two or more organisms living, for example, in a symbiotic community. Often one species could not survive on its own without its partner developing in an extremely accurate, mutually synchronised way at the same time. This renders the coincidental evolution of such crucial and mutually fitting characteristics for "foreign cohabitation partners" more than unlikely.

The English astronomer Fred Hoyle (1915-2001) once formulated the ironic metaphor of a Boeing 747: "The chance that evolution might have worked in the way we assume today is comparable to the chance that a tornado sweeping through a junkyard might assemble a Boeing 747 from the scrap material therein." Exactly my point of view.

Furthermore, modern biology takes the long-held view that everything characterising us is already determined by our genes, i.e. in our genetic material, and this applies equally to all plants, animals and humans.

It is easy so to argue when you have an *un*fathomable number of genes, since hardly conceivable numbers and quantities always serve well as knockout arguments. The same applies to the immense period of about

---

[27] Charles Darwin (1809-1882), English natural scientist and founder of the modern theory of evolution

half a billion years which many people mention to tip the scales when they want to substantiate the notion that evolution is the driving force behind all life on this earth.

In the 1990s, however, the American biochemist Craig Venter (*1946) indirectly put an end to this discussion: He established that humans only have 25-30 thousand genes which is much less than many plants or even yeasts have. Today we also know that the genes of humans and chimpanzees are identical to about 99% and that any human on this earth is to 99.9% genetically identical to any other human being.

Furthermore, many genes encode basically similar characteristics. For example, an FOXP2 gene in birds is responsible for their singsong and in humans for their ability to speak. The difference between the two is only marginal. And the so-called PAX6 gene encodes the eyes of insects as well as those completely different ones of mammals. When such a gene is implanted from a mouse, which has a lensed eye, into a fly, then a facet eye develops which is typical for insects.

Under sober consideration we must then assume that genes are more like a kind of folder containing numerous programs of the same category in the same way as we might have a file folder on our computer with "Photos" with several sub-folders such as "Travel" or "Family".

These folders specify which "tasks" or "tools" can be developed with the programs they may contain. However, depending on ingredients originating from "another source", these tasks or tools are then translated into completely different results. But what could "another source" mean here? Perhaps a comparison could help here. Take, for example, some roofers, they use the same tools and devices but with different "intellectual know-how and skills" and they construct different roofs in different ways.

It has been known for some years now that some processes in the brain can have an effect on the germ cells of a living being and thus even on subsequent generations. This effect has been proven experimentally in mice but also empirically in humans. For example, the grandchildren of people who had to go hungry during the Second World War are far more likely to suffer from eating disorders. By now, people can also imagine that large parts of our genetic material, which only some years ago were described as useless and superfluous, even as "genetic garbage", have, at least to some extent, important switch functions. Obviously processes which take place in whatever way within the brain can activate such switches via nerves (neuronal) or by hormones (hormonal) and thus precisely control new processes. Meanwhile we even have a term for this although we don't really know how it all works: "epigenetics".

Evolution and the Brain

I believe that epigenetics will enable us to progress much further over the next few years than we can imagine today. For me this seems to be a crucial "key" for a completely new understanding: For me epigenetics is the key to the recognition that each brain, as the supreme centre of the CNS in a sufficiently developed living being, is simultaneously the physical interface between spirit and body, i.e. between the world of information and the physical world.

Thus the brain even becomes a catalyst for evolution: An exponentially growing degree of interaction between the spirit and the brain influences the further evolution of the species, while the differentiation of the spirit coincides with that of its "equipment pool", the brain.

Here I go far beyond today's general appraisal of the brain: the brain of every living creature and thus primarily the human brain which has matured to a very high degree of complexity, is probably by no means the producer of everything spiritual as is almost universally assumed today.

In fact, each brain is, above all, a gigantic "equipment pool" with numerous "tools and devices" of very different kinds facilitating numerous capabilities and properties. Many of these devices are not first and foremost functioning as mere information storage as did (early versions of) computers. Of course, this is also part of their function but mainly on a "subordinate level". With good practice this feature can become beneficial whenever the spiritual influence would impede perfection , e.g. when driving a car or when playing musical instruments expertly. But in the same way as modern computers have long been equipped for high-speed access to the internet with its meanwhile gigantic amount of information, so are brains mainly meant to contact a purely "spiritual world" which exists in reality but remains for us purely spiritual.

The contact remains with us throughout our lives and improves continuously.

In the beginning it aims, in particular, to establish a personal and, of course, protected intranet similar to our own "cloud" on the internet. There we store everything, with its aid we depict ourselves and throughout our life we shape our significant share in it, individually and assuming large proportions simultaneously. Thus our very own, informational ("cloud") personality emerges and develops – a metaphor for our own increasingly complex maturing spirit. With the aid of its brain, this "non-physical spirit" has a constant informational and thus *non-energetic* connection with its own body.

Energetic interactions, which are repeatedly searched for but never found by physicists, no longer apply. I will come back to this in detail later. With the aid of their own spirit, each individual has potentially the opportunity to develop a "communication" and thus a real "exchange" with any other "spirit" or with other spiritual contents pertaining to the really existing and increasingly more complex world of information. As I have tried to explain in detail and argumentatively well-founded in my numerous books since the 1990s, the brain is an "interface" between spirit and body – or between a complex world of information and a complex physical world, as we perceive it with our senses. Through its "epigenetic action", as it is now termed, it thus grows into an increasingly more important force of evolution for its species in the course of time.

The brains of animals and humans, which are in constant interactive exchange, now even determine for their own species and in accordance with their individual degree of development, the direction of further developments.

34

The equipment pool "brain" becomes increasingly more varied in the course of its own evolution, the numerous devices become increasingly better in a "technical" sense and they can thus achieve ever more.

The brain as the crucial interface between the "spiritual world" and the "world of (finite) bodies" thus grows into an increasingly creative and more efficient force for the development of species and individuals which is no longer based on mere coincidence.

In this manner, the evolution of entire species moves into a completely new direction from time to time and experiences vigorous accelerations.

Coincidence and selection of the most suitable and the cooperation between the individual beings and species still remain to be important evolutionary mechanisms, of course. However, coincidence does not always result in positive developments: just think of the many (coincidental) mutations, which can afflict people on a daily basis and which not always improve their life but often kill them with diseases such as cancer if their immune system is unable to detect and eradicate them in time.

Evolution is mainly so successful in the long term because it deals with coincidence effectively. The neuronal system (CNS) with the brain at its apex has emerged over immense periods of time and developed slowly at first before progressing exponentially, much later becoming ever more interconnected and thus ever more important for this challenge. It serves specifically as an interface between the two polar-symmetrical worlds "information and matter"[28] and enables the constant and increasingly effective exchange of all necessary information between these two worlds. Over time, the evolution of life depends less and less on coincidence. The potentially dangerous coincidence is curbed and effectively reined in.

Evolution thus progresses from the lowest to every next higher level always in an increasingly orderly and purposeful manner.

---

[28] Here again we have two sides of one coin: While „information" is something absolute, matter is a relative concept and represents our perception of it as a way of expressing it.

However, it does not aim at humanity but rather an ever growing and ever more perfect spiritual complexity which is to a large degree merely represented in humans today.

This aim of the evolution of all life is actually *"info-trophic"* and has a *"neuro-trophic"* correlate which develops strictly linearly upwards in the physical world, i.e. the CNS with its complex brain at the apex, and it must be considered for its quantitative and qualitative properties. Hence humans today are only an intermediate stage. There are probably many more (spiritual) stages to be achieved, the contents and qualities of which we cannot at all fathom yet.

The decisive evolution, however, is a spiritual-informational one with its categorically linear upwards moving course aspiring to a new and higher order. It is the polar-symmetrical counterpart to a physical world which follows the law of entropy and thus strives to ever greater disorder.
The evolution of everything physical is ultimately merely a means to an end.
The spirit, maturing linearly with the aid of matter, also requires a linearly upwards developing physical correlate. Initially, therefore, a simple nervous system (NS) is created which over many millions of years develops further into ever more specialised centres and which moves linearly upwards to form the central nervous system (CNS).
This specialisation includes not only ever more new areas but also special qualities such as effective "reception areas".
In addition, the number of interconnections is also increasing exponentially over time. As the chosen interface between spirit and body the differentiation of the CNS is also moving linearly upwards and remains downwardly compatible in the same way as everything spiritual/informational. Every emergence and birth, development and growth up to the zenith as well as any decay, ageing and extinction or death of all (finite) objects and organs proceeds, of course, always in a cyclical manner just as everything physical in the entire universe does.
Of course, this also applies to the organ system "CNS" when it has fulfilled its duty as interface "at the end of its life". However, this in no

way applies to everything it has helped to get produced and achieved in the course of its existence.

While only a few decades ago animals were hardly attributed with relevant higher spiritual qualities such as intelligence or consciousness, we are often surprised today how some animal intelligence meets the highest expectations as has been proven by numerous experiments. The mental power of some animals is by far superior to that of toddlers; this applies, for example, to some birds, especially ravens with a comparatively puny brain. A core discipline, which even some schoolkids today seem to have lost, is clearly detectable in "lower animal forms": They master "elementary mathematics" to some degree. Fish can count low ordinal numbers and they recognise basic geometrical forms. In 2018 scientists at the Royal Melbourne Institute of Technology (*RMIT University*), Australia, were even able to teach honey bees simple addition and subtraction. Other insects can also count and even plants can do it as the carnivorous Venus flytrap proves.

Intelligence can also become evident in totally different ways. Dogs quickly learn to cooperate with other dogs if they can only get food by working together, even if then they do not have all the food for themselves. Herons learn entirely by themselves how to go fishing by observing children who feed the fish with breadcrumbs. They notice how many fish take the bait and come to the surface and they use "stolen bread" as bait themselves. They have obviously "understood" the process of effectively baiting fish with bread. This is only possible with sufficient intelligence. Some animals, such as chimpanzees, doubtless recognise themselves in a mirror.

Meanwhile there are countless examples which suggest that the seemingly obvious central and principal aim of evolution is the spiritual development of living beings.

In comparison to humans, evolutionary older animals are not yet as far developed spiritually; their CNS is still at a comparably lower level and must make do inferior devices". However, they often possess specific features which have been brought to perfection. Over time, however, the CNS reaches new and higher levels of development. Thus, the spiritual power grows slowly and gradually at first, and with an exponential growth rate later. Therefore, it only took us humans 400 generations to catapult us from the Stone Age, slowly at first, later with incredible speed, to our present era of modern technology. The brain, the physical basis of our spiritual development or, as I term it, the physical equipment pool, has not really changed since.

Casting a retrospective glance at the evolution of life, the former nervous system could be compared to an ancient valve radio.

It was able to receive necessary impulses but its performance was rather basic. With the CNS an already more complex system was created later: Similar to the more complex radio with an automatic record changer for 10 records and an old valve television set in a huge cupboard in the lounge, the latest craze during the 1950s, even the early CNS was capable of performing various and more sophisticated tasks. In addition, the variety of programmes grew, similar to radio and television programmes. Of course, this is just a metaphor and, in comparison, nature is by far superior to anything including us modern humans. The television set was eventually replaced by a computer, at the beginning without direct access to the outside world.

Later the first modems appeared. This allowed the first really interactive albeit still rather cumbersome, slow and very limited access to an "exterior data sphere". It contained little information, mainly rules and formatting.

For a long time, it still had to be enhanced with useful data: This is when the Internet first made its debut. Today it is constantly in use worldwide. Many people could not live without the Internet. Its wealth of data has grown exponentially and dramatically and it has become hardly comprehensible and understandable.

Almost everyone uses it creating with it and within it their own password protected areas, the intranet. We collect endless data, store ever more pictures and movies with relatively large data volumes increasingly using "Internet clouds". Of course, access to these clouds is growing more effective, increasingly faster in ever shorter periods of time. Interactive actions are suddenly fun, which can definitely not be said of the old BTX devices at the end of the 20th century.

All living beings on our earth are developing in a similar way, and – I am convinced of this – in countless other places throughout the entire universe, since this is also part of the inherent character of this world. We humans have only climbed the (temporary) peak of the iceberg since our CNS is a sufficiently matured equipment pool enabling us to operate interactively and for us to become aware of this. Our spirit has sufficiently matured for this. On the current developmental level of our CNS we are able to create our own "Intranet within this universal spiritual Internet", to extend it constantly and to identify it repeatedly. We *are* our "cloud" and we become aware of our own personality.

The currently achieved level of our spiritual development offers us not only self-awareness but in principle also the opportunity to make a move towards further knowledge. As Immanuel Kant already established we can only dedicate ourselves to understanding the "whole" by using our thoughts and our intellect. This should inevitably guide us to the absolute confidence that our "spiritual Intranet" is not identical with the brain which we only need "here" for its development as a physical interface and this spiritual Intranet will, therefore, not vanish. Death has no power over it!

Our personality does not die, *we* cannot die at all.

At the moment of our death, as it is termed here, our matured personality is our soul as we call it.

At the same moment a new life starts in a completely new dimension for which we do not yet possess any empirical values.

We hardly know anything about it, just as little as the twins in Henry Nouwen's "Dialogue of the Twins in the Womb", when they discuss their assumed imminent end, since they have no premonition as to what is waiting for them after their birth and they do not (cannot) know anything about it.

It is certain, however, that our soul will proceed consistently and *linearly* on its way to further advancement. I think we should consider a return to another terrestrial body at best to be a "tragic accident" in some isolated incidents but it is by no means the "usual case", contrary to what some religions and especially esoterics postulate, fantasising about innumerable cycles of reincarnations. Such accidents may then become manifest in certain mental disorders. Unfortunate recipients of such misguided souls might suffer from some forms of schizophrenia, especially from multiple personality disorder.

Such a reincarnation does not induce any further advancement. Rather, new mistakes are made and previous ones may not even be recognised and revised. But this contradicts all observations pertaining to the evolution of life and the consistently growing order of all information in the entire universe, which stands and must stand in polar-symmetrical contrast to the growing disorder (entropy) of all physical matter.

Having said that, social atrocities alone must be anathema to any spiritual advancement: It would mean that those "carnally reborn" people must blame themselves for their new and troublesome life due to their possible bad karma. Therefore, it would be better not to help here.

Size and mass of our brain are not the decisive factors for the developmental state of our spirit and its efficiency. It is hard to believe but even people who possess only about 10% of the normal brain mass are able to lead a normal and unremarkable life, as has been established by incidental findings in MRT examinations. And last but not least, various animals, including ravens and other birds, prove that even with a small brain you can perform intelligent tasks which are by no means inferior to those of a small child.

Much of the information seems not to be stored in detail in the brain. However, there seem to be traces of complex experiences which function in a similar manner to the genetic switches in the alleged garbage of our genetic material. If they are stimulated in whatever way – or "sharpened" – then the brain and, where necessary, the entire body is triggered into activity and a surge of emotion.

In 2015 at my seminar in Aachen Günter Haffelder (1940-2018), a brain researcher and Head of his "Institut für Kommunikation und Gehirnforschung" (Institute for Communication and Brain Research) in Stuttgart, who unfortunately died in the meantime, explained that especially strong and deep emotional experiences, such as states of medical anxiety but also complex near-death experiences induce very specific patterns in very low frequency brainwaves (in the delta and theta wavebands). In an EEG they can only be detected with the aid of special zoom techniques (Fourier analysis). These are virtual traces in the brain triggering memories which are not energetically stored there[29], but possibly on waves whose mathematical wave functions have a different ontological character and must be described by "hyper complex numbers" (Otte, R., 2018, see later).

Two studies carried out in 2009 and 2013 established that shortly after brain death is diagnosed and demonstrated by a zero line in the EEG, a resurgence of brain waves occurs for about 30 seconds.[30]
The majority of materialistic orientated brain researchers assumes that this is the long sought for physical correlate for the very multifaceted experiences in connection with near-death incidents and possibly also the proof for a present of evolution to the dying person.
Apart from the fact that such an idea is ludicrous especially on the basis of a materialistic ideology, it is essential for this gift to make sense in order to ensure the survival of the species. In this situation we can only laugh at such ideas. Moreover, such sudden activities of brainwaves *after* the actual brain death can also be found in experiments with rats. Should they and other animals also be rewarded with near-death experiences by nature at the end of their lives? For me this is utterly absurd!

However, there is something exceptional happening at this "farewell".
Not only single and scattered peaks of brainwaves are detected. No, the entire brain is literally hit by a proper electrical hurricane which sweeps in equal strength across all of its parts. If I evolve this idea a bit further I would conclude: This hurricane picks up everything that is stored in the brain in electrical and virtual patterns and takes it away. In fact, these studies support in fact my notion, which is widely

---

[29] Published in the relevant conference proceedings, 2016, "Schnittstelle Tod – Wo stehen wir nach 40 Jahren NTE-Forschung? See list of books at the end of this article.

[30] Chawla, I. et al. "Surges of Electoencephalogram Activity at the Time of Death: a Case Series", J. Palliative Med. 12(12), doi: 10.1ß89/jpm. 2009.0159 and Borijigin, J. et al. "Surge of neurophysilogical coherence and connectivity in the dying brain", doi: PNAS 10 (2013), doi: 10.1073/pnas 1316024110

supported by arguments from all fields of science, that in death we are sailing for new shores but we do not go under.

After all spirit AND brain!

Numerous observations seem to support my notion that spirit and brain are two lifelong very harmoniously cooperating partners which mutually influence and enhance each other. Although the brain is extremely elastic, i.e. it is able to react quickly and adequately to new requirements by creating a large number of newly interconnected cells, another fact that was completely unknown a few decades ago, it is nevertheless, as the "physical equipment pool", subject to physical (and thus energetic) basic principles.

Therefore, it always remains to be of finite nature. In contrast, with the aid of its brain the "non-physical" spirit can theoretically develop without any limits since information has no limits. These are also stored in the brain but by no means solely there.[31]

Finally the question arises, of course, as to how the spirit can affect the brain, if it is not, as is usually assumed today, a mere product of the brain, whereby the brain itself cannot be considered to be an impulse generator and initiator of thoughts, incentives, ideas, etc. and that it is by no means identical with ourselves and our EGO.

In accordance with all modern knowledge, we can with reasonable certainty dismiss the idea that there exists a conventional physical, i.e. energetic, interaction as René Descartes (1596-1650) once assumed.

In his book "Vorschlag einer Systemtheorie des Geistes" (engl. „Proposal of a System Theory of the Spirit", 2011 and 2016) the German engineer Ralf Otte, head of the "Institut für Künstliche Intelligenz und Automatisierungssysteme" (Institute for Artificial Intelligence and Automation Systems) at the TH Ulm (Technical

---

[31] Haffelder, G., "Nahtoderfahrung aus Sicht der Hirnforschung", NTE conference proceedings "Schnittstelle Tod – Wo stehen wir nach 40 Jahren NTE-Forschung?" 2016

University Ulm, Germany), made an alternative suggestion, what I believe to be a very plausible. He also gave a detailed presentation concerning this subject during my NTE-seminar in Aachen in 2017.[32] Professor Otte refers to the considerations of numerous authors, mine included as I already explained in 1999 and in several books at the beginning of the 2000s and sometimes similar ideas have been propounded by a number of other authors (e.g. 2002 and 2007 by the German physicist Thomas Görnitz; 2004 and 2005 by the US-American Henry Stapp (physics) and Jeffrey Schwartz (psychiatry); 2008 by the Dutch cardiologist Pim van Lommel; 2015 by the German Imre Koncsik (theology) and Ralf Krüger (psychiatry).

All these ideas, however, go back to John Eccles (1903-1997), the Australian brain researcher who is in my opinion the greatest brain researcher worldwide so far. In 1963 he was awarded the Nobel Prize for "Physiology or Medicine" for his research into the signal transmission via synapses in the brain. His discussions with the Austrian philosopher Karl Popper (1902-1994) – who was an agnostic for a long time – are not easily forgotten and they jointly published them in a book in 1977 (German edition 1982).[33]

In his marvellous book "Evolution of the Brain" (1989) – published in German in 1994 under the title "Wie das Selbst Sein Gehirn steuert" – Eccles was the first ever to point out the actual microanatomy of the outer cerebral cortex which is still largely ignored by most brain researchers.

From this research he derived the notion that a brain-*independent* spirit could possibly govern the brain by quantum processes, an idea which was absolutely revolutionary and very provocative in the 1970s.

In the brain as everywhere else in the body, information is transmitted via nerves. This information is transmitted electrically, although today

---

[32] Otte, R. "Physikalische Grundalgen des Geistes", NTE conference proceedings "Schnittstelle Tod – Sind Religionen religiös und Wissenschaften wissend?", 2018

[33] Eccles, J.C., Popper, K., "The Self and its Brain" (1977); "Das Ich und sein Geist (1982)

other ideas must also at least be discussed (e.g. "mechanical pressure wave").[34]

Nerves latch on to either other nerves or to a (successful) organ or a muscle. The point of contact is termed synapse. There the *electrical* impulse is very nearly always transmitted *chemically* by means of certain substances (so-called transmitters, neurotransmitters, transfer agents, chemical messengers). The transmitters are released by small vesicles located near a synapse. They then cross the very narrow "synaptic gap" and stimulate, for example, the next nerve on the other side which results in a new *electrical* impulse. Thus synapses are in general there to help transmit an electrical impulse from one anatomical structure to another. In the brain, however, there are countless billions of nerve endings near the outer upper cortex which are simply extending freely upwards and do not latch on to anything else. These in turn are covered with trillions of vesicles which are distributed throughout the brain and, although they all contain transmitters, they do not transmit impulses from one nerve to the next. But why does the cerebrum possess such a gigantic number of "blind ending" nerves? What could affect them and induce them to release their countless transmitters? What could trigger impulses in them when no other nerve is interconnected and eligible for this?

John Eccles had the fantastic idea that this could be the interface between spirit and brain.
He compared the many trillions of vesicles to smallest parabolic mirrors which could receive information.
He was thinking of photons, i.e. smallest (light) quanta, and he wondered whether a brain-*independent* spirit could possibly control the brain by quantum processes. However, if they are measured they are energetic. Thus, the problem of interaction is not solved.

Ralf Otte demonstrated, however, that the parallelism of both worlds "spirit and matter" can be solved mathematically and can be exactly

---

[34] Heimburg, T. "Das Mechanische Gehirn", in the magazine "Spektrum der Wissenschaft 9 2018

described scientifically, and this for both the physical world of tissue by quantum mechanics and for the spiritual world of the mental by developing a special information mechanics which is based on hyper-complex wave functions. For details, please refer to the publications I have already mentioned.

But how can the spiritual world then influence the physical world?
Quantum physics tells us that the physical world is governed solely by coincidence. By no means do we decide whether Schrödinger's cat will live or die when we open its cave. Either it is alive or dead.
As I already mentioned, coincidences will time and again result in a new order in the physical world if the period of time is sufficiently *long*. Therefore, we must develop this idea further.
Since 1999 I have repeatedly demonstrated in numerous books that our entire universe seems to strive towards an ever more complex order of information or, in other words, towards spiritualisation which is, moreover, widely distributed over as many shoulders as possible.
In general terms and with prosaic words we could say that initially simple information strives for *ever more* and simultaneously *increasingly complex* information clusters.
Or, to express it in the style of good marketing:
Maximum perfection of the spirit in simultaneously maximum diversity.

However, humanity is not the aim (not on our earth either), as many people believe when they speak of an "anthropic principle". No, the ultimate aim is the *spirit* that is advancing in its development in parallel with the physical equipment pool "CNS" which is perfected at the same time and aids its development. This is why I talked decades ago already of the "*neurotropic principle*" – and in connection with this and in general – of an "*infotropic principle*" as being the aim of the evolution of the whole universe.

In physics, coincidence is the first and crucial driving force for everything including, of course, the evolution of the universe. This is exactly why every development initially requires immense periods of time before a significant progress is detectable. Meanwhile we are

45

familiar with such immense periods of time although in reality they are probably unfathomably longer than the 13.8 billion years so far assumed to have passed since the Big Bang.

In contrast, our modern spirit is developing comparatively rapidly with the aid of its physical correlate, the human brain. This demonstrates that even the most complex developments in nature can proceed at a much greater speed in the end, presumably BECAUSE evolution strives relatively early on to make coincidence, its first and most important driving force, redundant.

As I already mentioned, it took evolution about 40 million years to develop hooves. For developing the human cerebrum, in comparison, it only needed a few hundred thousand years. And the spiritual development, from ancient Stone Age people about 10,000 years ago up to modern human beings of the information age has progressed with breath-taking speed in comparison, without implementing any new devices in the hardware of the brain – with all of today's known advantages and disadvantages, since everything has two polar-symmetrical sides like Yin and Yang.

On the basis of all our so far acquired knowledge and without the arrogance of many scientists and even more opinion-forming media and without ignoring the innumerable "metaphysical" experiences worldwide, we must revise our thinking. Professor Otte from Ulm then proposed a very plausible theory:[35]
In my conference proceedings of 2018 he writes: " ... spiritual processes also can only intervene in the order of physics by random processes ... (This is, by the way, exactly the reason why these effects are so difficult to detect). But an influence caused by random processes can produce a pseudo-causality. In "normal physics" this will go unnoticed (apart from

---

35 Otte, R. "Physikalische Grundlagen des Geistes" In the conference proceedings 2018 "Schnittstelle Tod – Sind Religionen religiös und Wissenschaften wissend?", which is based on his book "Vorschlag einer Systemtheorie des Geistes, Culliver (2016)

it being accepted that coincidence happens there as well), in highly interconnected systems, however, a quasi-causal process is possible ..."

This is exactly the decisive factor: In the inanimate universe of the physical world coincidence alone always decides initially. It often forces any evolution to spend immensely long periods of time before anything at all evolves which is then developed in "undisturbed calmness and temporal composure". At some point, however, "living systems" emerge and soon enough "neuronal-interconnected communication systems" are generated, such as (simple) nervous systems and later central nervous systems.

All physical matter is structured discontinuously, i.e. it is quantised. It always consists of individual particles. Thereby something completely new is generated: These discontinuous structures of living systems now start to interconnect, gradually and slowly at first and then increasingly faster and ever more complex. In the course of time, huge networks emerge everywhere even on the lowest level of living systems, i.e. of living beings.

This brings us back to the billions upon billions of nerve fibres extending upwards in the human cerebral cortex. John Eccles already pointed them out with emphasis. They carry billions of vesicles which are not simply floating around freely. Rather, they are carefully arranged in special grids (so-called vesicle grids), comparable to egg trays for 30 or more eggs. Each individual vesicle contains transmitter substances. The chemical messengers are thus neatly arranged and from there they activate nerves and trigger new electrical impulses which are then transmitted. However, there are no nerve endings latching on to them "from the outside" – they are dead-ended. So why are they there in this immense quantity? Eccles referred to them as small parabolic mirrors for the reception of information.

Thoughts could generate quantum processes, according to Ralf Otte's suggestions, and could then accidentally burst the vesicle which are so tightly arranged in the grid like eggs in a tray.

These would then drain and release chemical messengers. Consequently, this would result in a "first stimulation" of the nerve endings in the brain which are connected "downwards". This electrical "first impulse" would then be transmitted in the known way. This "first exertion of influence" by the "spirit" must also be explained by coincidence, to exclude any inadmissible energetic interactions.

But should it only be possible for us to lift our arm coincidentally after our thoughts expressed the will to do so? Of course not.

Hence, we must consider how a spiritual influence by pure coincidence immediately leads to the "desired" order and not only after a long period of time as is usually the case in the physics of inanimate matter.

The immense networks offer us a solution:

Do you play the lottery? With 6 numbers out of 49 you have the choice of about 14 million combinations without taking the bonus number into consideration. Therefore, it is highly unlikely that you will select the exact 6 "correct" numbers which correspond with the drawn numbers, because this is what you have to do if you want to win the jackpot.

Let us assume now, that there are 100 vesicles in a vesicle grid, just like eggs in a full egg tray, of which only 10 must drain *randomly* in order to drain the entire grid at once and to fire an initial electrical impulse. There are now more than 17 trillion possibilities.

But in this metaphor, in contrast to the lottery game, it is completely irrelevant which of the vesicles burst. If the 6 numbers you select in the lottery did not matter either you would be a millionaire every week. Wouldn't that be just great?

This means that only 10 of the assumed 100 vesicles per grid must burst to release messenger substances and trigger an electrical impulse.

In a similar way, even one single thought could already have a targeted effect on the brain by randomly triggered quantum processes.

But perhaps it would be necessary for several vesicles to burst simultaneously and release transmitters. This would increase the thresholds.

However, with such short odds of scoring a hit it would still be easy to score – and that is in fact the case as we experience every single day.

If we now further assume, as Ralf Otte wrote in his contribution to my conference proceedings 2018, that 1,000 nerves (neurons) must in fact be activated briefly and simultaneously in order to lift an arm as desired. Only then the arm – and any other process – would be set into motion via the corresponding centres of the cerebral cortex (motoric cortex and others). Now they are all interconnected in a neuronal network. Let us now also assume that the stimulation of 100 random neurons should be sufficient in this example to "ignite" all 1,000 nerves simultaneously. There are then 6.3×10^{139} possibilities and thus probably more than our universe has atoms according to our current knowledge.

Hence, the probability concerning the stimulation of any random nerves by pure coincidence now turns into an almost "deterministic necessity" due to their extremely high degree of interconnections. The first example demonstrates the "systematic stimulation" of a dead-ended nerve ending on the outer cerebral cortex which is initially indeed coincidental but already provoked by the special "composite arrangement" in the same vesicle grid. This underlines the notions of Eccles and much later Otte that information induced by coincidental quantum-physical processes, here a single thought or in general the spirit, can affect the brain rapidly and systematically.

In the physical world of inanimate nature unbelievably *immense periods of time* are the key for the effect of information and thereby the development of order due to coincidences.

In animate systems, however, the continuously *growing interconnection* plays this key role right from the start – and it works far more quickly and very soon it influences further evolution. The next level of evolution is the real "quantum leap": In animate systems "neuronal-interconnected systems" are generated and they develop rapidly in extreme numbers. This saves a lot of time since now specific highly complex "neuronal clusters" are generated which help to govern further evolution. In humans they culminate in the "cerebrum" which is the youngest part of the brain. Even this is surely not the peak of development ...

Now we come to the point I have explained in detail in my numerous earlier books ever since 1999:

The crucial basis of our world is the "spirit" or the "spiritual principle".
Spirit is *originally the basis of everything and affects everything,* since

spirit soon creates the necessary path for itself to achieve this by way of evolution and the development of corresponding evolutionary mechanisms. The aim of the "spiritual principle" as the basis of this world is ultimately the consistent and steady "own" differentiation towards an ever higher degree of perfection in a maximum possible diversity. This alone requires a "second level", the known world of physical objects. And another reason renders this even mandatory: Especially in order to achieve "maximum diversity" it becomes necessary that time and again ever "new spirits" are given the chance to live.

Thus we hold the key in our hands to the acceptance of the real existence of a brain-*independent* spirit which can survive our death at the end of our life as a matured "soul" and which, as I maintain, indeed does and must survive it, of course!

Summary, Conclusion and Outlook

Our world, the entire universe, simply everything, and we ourselves who are a small and yet very important part of one unimaginable whole entity are definitely cast from one single mould.

Since time immemorial we have asked ourselves metaphysical questions such as: Is there a creative intelligence? Is there a God irrespective of what we want to call "him or she or it"? Is there a spirit, a spiritual dimension? And, of course, does our life end with death? Do we humans have a free will? What is our "Self"?

Are life and spirit mere coincidental products of matter?

Is our universe really the result of a Big Bang?

We will certainly all be confronted with these questions and many more somehow at some time or other.

Natural sciences and religions often have differing and sometimes even mutually exclusive arguments.

Natural sciences and some related disciplines all too often continue to insist on notions which are reduced to materialism (naturalism) alone.

"God" and a "brain-independent spirit" have no place here, nor does our "Self" and a – at least in principle – "free will", let alone the belief that we survive our death which is at best smiled upon as "naïve romanticism".

Although many religions, often institutionalised today, have in principle evolved on the basis of such "metaphysical" questions since time immemorial, they have nevertheless developed doctrines therefrom in the course of long periods of time, mostly incomprehensible, with wide ramifications and often hardly corresponding or even just complementing each other.

Their doctrines gather everything that is in some way human. They are mostly influenced by all conceivable notions of every age since their beginnings. Of course, any of these doctrines is solely the work of humans. No "God" has invented them.

A closer look at our world ought to go beyond the various horizons of different affected disciplines. An analysis of all relevant sciences and disciplines should simultaneously avoid any arrogance and ignorance with regard to the many subjective metaphysical experiences which in some cases can even be confirmed objectively.

In the end I have arrived at the following conclusion for decades:

Everything in our world and thus the whole universe is subject to really existing laws which are of elementary mathematical and especially geometrical nature. They form the basic parameters for every development. They are at the core of the "powers" of nature and they also control all mysterious "relationships", for example those between particles which we then perceive in a small section of this world which we call the physical world.

Everything in this world has two sides, one of which being the stronger one and serving as a "kind" of primordial basis for everything. The other one derives from the first one. Of course, they are both closely related on all levels and they mutually influence each other. For me, the ancient and probably wise Chinese symbolism of Yin and Yang characterises these interconnections very aptly.

The primordial basis for all describable and really perceivable existence is the world of information or of the spirit which includes the mathematical basic parameters already mentioned.

Since the beginning of time, it has continuously been on the journey to itself. More precisely, it is on the *linear* path to its own maximum differentiation (perfection) in maximum possible diversity.

For this purpose – and also especially on account of the required diversity – a further part is mandatory. We term this part the "physical world". Since we ourselves and also all our devices, however large or small, reaching from the telescope to the microscope, always obey the structure in accordance with the fixed laws of this physical world, we have major problems in recognising and accepting the reality which exceeds it and simultaneously substantiates it. The latter is mainly the result of what I call scientific arrogance today.

The second, the physical part of the world, which we call the world of matter, has been generated by the first and has ever since been governed by it and is "interconnected" in the entire universe.

We then interpret a section of such "informational" interconnections incorrectly as a mere manifestation of matter.

This also applies to the interpretation of physical particles, such as massless particles of information or, generally speaking, photons, as being simultaneously also waves (wave-particle dualism in physics).

The same applies to the, in my opinion, ridiculous interpretation of our spirit as being the mere product or epiphenomenon of the brain.

Furthermore, an alternative perspective explains with ease and sophistication all natural phenomena which we can indeed describe today with mathematical precision but about which we still do not know why they are interconnected and why they work.

Finally, this also includes such mysterious physical phenomena as the remote influence of entangled particles.

We humans are a part of both worlds like everything else in the universe, just like every smallest particle of which, from a physical perspective, we are made after all. Of course, no single atom possesses consciousness, but consciousness is part of us since it is in itself also a result of the evolution of the essence, of the spirit or of a world of information by harnessing the physical world which has emerged with it and from it. In my novel "Our key to Eternity" (2015) I chose the image of a watermill as a simple metaphor for this. It raises water from a lower level to a higher level. And in a similar way the "spiritual world" needs its "physical world" in order to progress steadily, becoming faster, better and more focussed by evolving the physical world at first and then developing together with it, indirectly and for the long term.

In the course of our life our consciousness strives – in principle just like everything informational– *linearly* upwards to ever higher complexity. Only our physical brain can jeopardise this development by way of "hardware failure" such as dementia or Alzheimer's disease since it is subject to *cyclical entropy,* i.e. to the pursuit of ever greater disorder, like all physical systems. Our conscious spirit may then lose control over its equipment pool which throughout its life had been so useful.

At the end of its physical life, which is subject to the *cyclical* laws of physics, its physical death is, of course, the final point of "entropy". However, this does not apply to the spirit which has matured linearly up to this point.
The spirit survives its body in death and that without any break in its perspective. Its personality, matured up until then and surviving death, is the "soul". It is immortal seeking new horizons of which we do not and cannot have the faintest idea, just as unborn children can have no notion of what is awaiting them.

This is why it is so immensely important for all humans today to adjust their lives accordingly, since eventually very important assignments await every individual in an unfathomably different world. This will also and especially include our humbly seeking forgiveness for our own misdemeanours and our granting it to others likewise. For this reason, the only crucial maxim, often referred to as "Golden Rule of Ethics" applies to us here and throughout the universe at all times: "Do not do to other people what you do not want others to do to you."

Current Books by Prof. Dr. Walter van Laack in English:

1. Novel:

Our Key To Eternity,
ISBN 978-3-936624-18-2 (SC), 308 p. (2016),
ISBN 978-3-936624-31-1, E-Book (2016)

2. Non-fiction Books

Keystones Of Our World: The Whole World Is Information
ISBN 978-3-936624-33-5 (SC), 68 p. (2016)
ISBN 978-3-936624-34-2, E-Book (2016)

To Perceive The World With Logic
ISBN 978-3-936624-08-3, (SC), 340 p. (2007),
ISBN 978-3-936624-09-0, E-Book (2008)

Nobody Ever Dies!
ISBN 978-3-936624-03-8, (SC), 272 p. (2005),
ISBN 978-3-936624-22-9, E-Book (2013)

A Better History of Our World

Vol. 1, "The Universe"
ISBN 978-3-8311-1490-0, (SC), 188 p. (2001)

Vol. 2, "Life"
ISBN 978-3-8311-2597-5, (SC), 236 p. (2002)

Vol. 3, "Death"
ISBN 978-3-936624-01-4, (SC), 276 p. (2003)

Key To Eternity
ISBN 978-3-8311-0344-7, (SC), 256 p. (2000)

3. Bilingual non-fiction "Upside-Down" Book-Series:

"Lectures & Insights – Vorträge & Einsichten"

**Dying and Death from a Scientific Point of View &
Sterben und Tod aus wissenschaftlicher Sicht**
(Vol. 1)
ISBN 978-3-936624-41-0, Softcover (SC), 44 p. (2018) 5,00 €
ISBN 978-3-936624-42-7, E-book (2018)

**World views yesterday and today –
What will remain and what will be laughed at tomorrow?
& Weltbilder gestern und heute –
Was bleibt und worüber lacht man morgen?**
(Vol. 2)
ISBN 978-3-936624-49-6 (will be published shortly)

**World views yesterday and today –
What will remain and what will be laughed at tomorrow?**
(Vol. 2 , only English-Version)
ISBN 978-3-936624-47-2 (SC), 56p. (2020) 5,00 €

**These and several other books are also available
in German language.**

Please visit my book-websites:
www.vanLaack-Buch.de & www.vanLaack-Book.eu

van Laack GmbH, Aachen,
Book-Publishers
(HRB-Aachen 5584)

Managing Director: Prof. Dr. Walter van Laack
Board: Dr.-Ing. Dipl.-Wirt.-Ing. Alexander van Laack,
Martin van Laack, M.Sc., Prof. Dr. Walter van Laack

Roermonder Str. 312, D- 52072 Aachen
Fax: +49-3212-9319310
Web: www.vanLaack-Book.eu – www.vanLaack-Buch.de
Email: webmaster(at)van-Laack.de

Supplied by:
Book-on-Demand (BoD)
In de Tarpen 42, D- 22848 Norderstedt, Fax +49-40-534335-84
Web: www.bod.de   Email: info(at)bod.de